CW00660024

Middlesbrough
in old picture postcards

Robin Cook

European Library   ZALTBOMMEL/THE NETHERLANDS

A Present
for my mate
Bret 19/11/2014.

BACK IN TIME

GB ISBN 90 288 2806 0

© 1984 European Library – Zaltbommel/The Netherlands

Eighth edition, 2000: reprint of the original edition of 1984.

European Library

post office box 49

NL – 5300 AA Zaltbommel/The Netherlands

telephone: 0031 418 513144

fax: 0031 418 515515

e-mail:publisher@eurobib.nl

INTRODUCTION

This book does not pretend to be a history book about Middlesbrough and the immediate district. Over the past hundred years, others better qualified have recorded the spectacular growth and development of the area from the early part of the nineteenth century. It is however a reflection of that history, in the form of postcards and a few photographs which capture scenes from the early part of this century. No doubt many of the old postcards, as today, were thrown away within weeks of being purchased and used, but thankfully a representative selection has survived.

I am particularly indebted to the local collectors named elsewhere, without whose help this book could not have been produced. Putting together 140 interesting and high quality scenes cannot be achieved by any one collector without the help of others, and I very much appreciate the trust and confidence placed in me by them. I hope that they feel that the end product has justified their faith and cooperation!

The golden age of the postcard was the period from the beginning of the century up to the Great War — i.e. 1900 to 1914. Millions of cards were produced, and the message on the back of those which survive often includes the remark: 'Here's another one for your collection.' There was a national craze which did not confine itself to local views, but which ranged over virtually every imaginable subject. Although Middlesbrough was not conventionally photogenic, thank goodness that there were local and national postcard manufacturers who wanted to capture the events and scenes of that period in this area. The collection which follows tries to reflect many different aspects of the district as it was so long ago, and I very much hope that the enthusiasm of the collectors for these views is shared by the readers.

Many of the cards were produced by local firms, including Brittain and Wright, and Heavisides, of Stockton; Sanbride (Hoods), RSK (Kirkpatrick), James Dodds, T.W. Campling and Haig Parry of Middlesbrough, and Monarch (Johnston) of Gateshead. There are also many from the national firms of the day, like Valentine in particular, Frith, Wrench, Photocrom, and Rotary Photographic. Several have no attribution, and are likely to owe their origins to keen local amateurs who saw an interesting scene and had the initiative to capture it for posterity.

Without venturing here into the history of Middlesbrough as a serious topic, it is clear that the rate of development of the town during the second half of the nineteenth century was exceptional by any standards, although subject as ever to the fluctuating fortunes of the main industry around which it grew. A sense of civic pride emerged early, and this is also evident from the events and buildings captured in the following selection. The town's first phase, from 1830, lay around the riverside due to the sea traffic in exporting coal. This obliged its later development to be to the south. Original villages became suburbs, and then part of the town itself, as new suburbs were created. I have tried to devote due attention to all the main focal points as they emerged — the old town 'beyond the railway tracks' and the riverside; the railway station and Albert Road; the 'new' Town Hall area and Corporation Road; Newport Road; Linthorpe Road; North Ormesby and Cargo Fleet; Linthorpe Village, and Acklam. I have also briefly included South Bank, Ormesby and Marton, but have left out Grangetown, Eston, Normanby, and Nunthorpe, from the present selection.

If this publication gives as much pleasure to the reader as it did to me in compiling it, then I will feel that the effort has been very well worthwhile.

ACKNOWLEDGEMENTS

In addition to using items from my own collection, I am indebted to the following friends for the loan of their original postcards, and, in a few instances, of old photographs:
John Armstrong; Reverend Philip Battersby; Araf Chohan; Jeanne Dobson; the Dorman Museum; Fred Gilbert; Carol Hunter; Joan Lambert; Les Matthews; Valentine Sagar; Len Whitehouse and Reverend Bill Wright.

Thanks are also due to Peter Dobing for photographic assistance, and to Sue Mahoney for typing the complete text.

I have found 'The History of Middlesbrough', written by the late William Lillie — the Borough Librarian for twenty-five years up to 1951 — particularly helpful for some of the factual information. His book was first published in 1968. Various other directories and reference books have also proved useful.

V392-9   MIDDLESBOROUGH. MARKET PLACE.   RAPID PHOTO. E.C.

1. An interesting view of the Market Place in the old town. In the foreground is a pot stall, behind which can be seen a tripe stall with the product clearly visible. Just beyond the stall on the right a small crowd is listening to the patter of a man in a straw boater. The Market Buildings on the right are no longer standing, but a more modern building housing a health clinic has replaced them under the clock tower. The highest, rear section of the buildings in the centre of the Square was the original Town Hall, built in 1846. Mr. Gladstone was received in this building on 9 October 1862, when on an official visit to the town. The building is now used as a branch library.

Market Place and Parish Church Middlesbrough

2. St. Hilda's Parish Church was completed in 1840, having been built on part of the site of the original Priory Church of Benedictine Monks, dating back to the twelfth century. Public subscriptions raised most of the money for the church, and the land was given by Joseph Pease and the Owners of the Middlesbrough Estate, providing that two pews were reserved for their use and that the spire was at least 120 feet high. Roundabouts were a regular feature in the Market Place — this one is William Murphy's 'most popular riding machine of the day', in the year 1907.

Parish Church, Middlesbrough

3. An interior view of St. Hilda's with the old 'box' pews clearly illustrated. A gallery — from which this view was taken — was added to the church in 1861. The building was demolished in 1969-70.

4. A typical back street view in the old town, this being taken in Hilda Place, just by St. Hilda's Church, in 1910. A row of outside toilets can be seen on the left, with a pair of 'poss' tubs on the right and a poss stick visible. The children are barefoot.

5. The Coronation of King George V took place on 22 June 1911. The Middlesbrough celebrations were organised by the Deputy Town Clerk — Preston Kitchen — and the ox-roasting occurred under a special canopy in the Market Place. The children received medals, chocolates and sweets, and a very large procession ended at Albert Park, with entertainments and fireworks.

6. The Coronation ox was prepared for consumption by Mr. J.H. Wray, and the roasting began on the evening of 21 June. For a shilling the public were given a piece of roasted ox on a special commemorative plate. Alternatively, at a cost of 2d., an ox sandwich was provided. The ox had been given free by the tradesmen in the old town, and the proceeds were used for giving the old people a tea in the Market Hall, and providing a seaside trip to Redcar for 1,000 children on the following 6 August.

South Street and Market Hall, Middlesbrough

7. A scene from South Street in the old town, with the Market Hall and Parish Church in the distance. Taken in the summer, judging by the shop awnings and shadows. Pottage's, the shop to the right, was a drapers and outfitters. The sender of the card explains that she is going to Redcar Races on the following day.

8. The original Amos Hinton 'grocer, tea dealer and provision merchant's' shop in the old part of Middlesbrough, in South Street. A delivery cart stands outside, and a male shop assistant stands in clean white apron in the doorway on the right. Taken about 1890. Amos Hinton took over this business in 1871.

DACRE ST. POLICE STATION.
STONEWORK SUPPLIED BY BOLCKOW VAUGHAN & CO.LTD.
S.E.BURGESS, BOROUGH ENGINEER, MIDDLESBROUGH.

9. Dacre Street Police Station, an imposing building which still stands today in old Middlesbrough. It has not been used for its original purpose for many years, and is now a Community Launderette. The card, issued by S.E. Burgess, the Borough Engineer, was an advertising item for Bolckow and Vaughan's artificial stonework, made from slag from the iron works. A number of similar cards were issued showing various projects in which their building products had been used. A very large building – 70 yards by 20 yards – containing a butchers' market existed previously in the area of this site, with space for 150 butchers stalls, according to Kelly's 1887 directory.

BLAST FURNACES, MIDDLESBROUGH.

10. A view of the Linthorpe Iron Works, which was in the Ironmasters District close to the old town. The Riverside Park Industrial Estate is now being developed on the site of these blast furnaces. Probably taken about 1915.

11. A view taken about 1910 in one of the local steelworks — probably the Acklam Works. Some idea of the heavy nature of the work is captured by the photographer. Lady Bell's 'At the Works', originally published in 1907, creates a powerful impression of the life of the steelworkers and their families in Middlesbrough.

MIDDLESBROUGH FERRYBOAT.

No 711.

12. The 'Erimus' ferry boat, built by Raylton Dixon and Company, was launched in 1888 and could carry more than 900 passengers. The first large ferry carrying horses and carts as well as passengers on the Middlesbrough to Port Clarence crossing came into service in 1874. With the Transporter Bridge opening in 1911, the last two ferry boats – the 'Erimus' and the 'Hugh Bell' – were sold to a Southampton company in 1912.

13. A river scene — taken from a glass negative — of the early stages of construction of the Transporter Bridge. A special temporary anchoring tower was constructed on each bank of the river, in order to hold the permanent towers in position until the bridge was completed. This can be seen as the vertical girders on the extreme right hand. Picture taken during 1910.

The Transporter Bridge, Middlesbrough.

14. An interesting view of an incomplete Transporter Bridge — the centre span is not quite linked together. The card dates from early 1911, when the ferry service was still operating. Taken from the north bank of the river at Port Clarence, this view also shows operating coal staithes, with a rake of rail wagons on a raised track.

15. The opening ceremony of the Transporter Bridge, which took place on 17 October 1911. His Royal Highness Prince Arthur of Connaught performed the opening, and most of the local nobility appear to have attended. Note the special viewing platform in the girders on the left hand side. The total cost of the bridge was just over £87,000.

16. After lunch at the offices of the Tees Conservancy Commissioners in Queens Square, Prince Arthur, escorted by the mounted Yorkshire Hussars, travelled to Albert Park, which had been opened by his father, the Duke of Connaught, in 1868. The Prince planted a tree in the Park, and then went on to open the Kirby School. A banquet was held in the Town Hall in the evening.

17. An early view of the Transporter Bridge in operation, with the travelling car neatly framed by the tower structure. The Bridge Superintendent stands at the right hand end of the upper deck. Unlike the present time – when the Transporter is working – the car has only pedestrians on board.

AIR VIEW OF TRANSPORTER BRIDGE. MIDDLESBOROUGH

18. An aerial view taken from near the Transporter Bridge and showing some of the heavy industry lying close to the river in the old part of Middlesbrough. This view was taken in the 1920's.

RIVER TEES, FROZEN OVER, CHRISTMAS DAY 1860 TO MARCH 1861.

N° 612.

19. It is popularly believed that winters were more severe in the distant past. The Tees was apparently frozen over on a number of occasions in the eighteenth and nineteenth centuries. There was skating on the river at Newport on Christmas Day 1860, and several times in January 1861. Other years when the river froze over were 1780 and 1784. In the latter year a sheep was roasted on the river at Portrack on St. Valentine's Day. This sailing vessel was stranded by the ice on the river, which apparently lasted from Christmas 1860 until the following March.

The Harbour Mouth, Middlesbro'.

20. An interesting scene along the river, with two paddle-driven tugs. The 'Harbour Mouth' is at Dock Point, which is ahead at the end of the promenade. Taken about 1910.

MIDDLESBOROUGH. FURNACES FROM DOCK POINT.

21. Furnaces by the riverside opposite Dock Point. Two paddle tugs are moored on the far bank, and the timberyard of the Owners of the Middlesbrough Estate is to the right. Dock Point was clearly a place to which people came to admire the view!

39885. MIDDLESBROUGH. THE DOCKS.

22. A busy scene at the dockside in 1910, with coal wagons in the foreground, and two steam locomotives awaiting transit. This card was sent to his girlfriend in Deauville, France, by an officer from the S/S 'Palermo', then docked in Middlesbrough.

IN MIDDLESBRO DOCKS   Nº 219.

23. A three-masted ship in the Middlesbrough Dock, surrounded by the usual array of interesting cranes. Posted in 1910, the card features the 'Caradoc', registered at Aberystwyth. The provision of proper docking facilities was originally proposed in 1837, and excavation work began early in 1840. The dock opened for business in May 1842, and extensions were made in 1869, 1885 and 1898.

24. An interesting view of coal loading from rail wagons to ship in the Middlesbrough Dock, the ship being the 'Flodden' of West Hartlepool. A second coal hoist can just be seen in the distance on the original postcard, and the clock tower is on the right. Taken about 1910.

THE DOCKS, MIDDLESBOROUGH, FROM THE AIR

25. A good aerial view of the Middlesbrough Dock — which closed within the last few years — when in full action. Fourteen large cargo ships can be seen, as well as hundreds of associated railway wagons. Probably taken about 1930. Dock Point is just off the top of the picture.

Queen's Square, Middlesbro'

26. A general view of Queens Square, with the roadway being of cobbled structure, and the tramway passing through to the riverside. The Erimus Club (now replaced by Erimus House) and the Seamen's Institute (now replaced by Teesdale House) are on the right. The Tees Conservancy Commissioners Offices (built in 1899) are on the left, and the splendid National Provincial Bank of England premises (built in 1872) are in the distance.

27. St. Nicholas' Seamen's Church and Institute, in Queens Square, opened in 1895, having taken over the premises – originally built in 1856 – from the Congregational Church. Recreation facilities were provided at the Institute for visiting seamen, and sleeping accommodation was offered in Gosford Street (which lies behind the photographer). The horse-drawn gentlemen's carriages stand outside the Erimus Club building, frequented by the leading businessmen of the town and erected in 1873. The tramway lines can just be seen running across the foreground of the picture.

P.C. 39889 Middlesborough. Albert Road.

28. Albert Road in the leisurely days of horse and cart. The card was posted in 1908. The tram is heading for the Transporter Bridge. Albert Road has clearly been the business centre of the town for at least the whole of the twentieth century. The shop on the right hand side with the white awnings is the original Newhouses, a drapers business which began in these premises in 1890.

29. The first electric tram, probably seen here on the opening day of the system run by the Imperial Tramways Company of Bristol — 16 July 1898. Tremendous interest was aroused. This scene is at the junction of Corporation Road and Albert Road, and the tram is travelling towards North Ormesby Road. Most of the passengers look particularly elegant, and the curtains are partly drawn on the far side of the lower deck. The Company locally was called the Middlesbrough, Thornaby and Stockton Electric Tramways.

Middlesboro'. Corporation Road.

30. Posted in August 1907, this card shows an open tram driving towards Grange Road, having just passed Hinton's shop on its left — note the Amos Hinton advertisement on the tram! A lady in a long dress rides carefree on a bicycle in the distance. The town looks very quiet on this occasion.

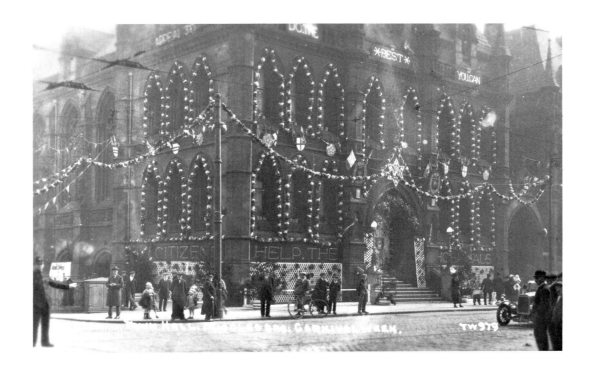

31. The main entrance to the Town Hall in 1925, during Carnival Week, when an appeal was being made for the citizens to give generously to the hospitals. Each of the windows is surrounded by garlands, which are also festooned from the standards supporting the tram wires.

32. Waving to the crowds as he descends the Town Hall steps after a special lunch, H.R.H. the Prince of Wales (later briefly Edward VIII and subsequently the Duke of Windsor) visited Middlesbrough on 2 July 1930. He is seen here accompanied by Sir Hugh Bell, the Lord Lieutenant. The Prince had come to open the new Constantine Technical College, of which more than £50,000 of the total cost had been contributed by the Constantine family from their shipping fortunes.

33. Another Albert Road view, with the Town Hall and Amos Hinton's premises to the right, and the Corporation Hotel and the shop of Freeman, Hardy & Willis to the left.

34. A good close-up of the unveiling of the Sir Samuel Sadler memorial statue on 21 June 1913, in Victoria Square behind the Town Hall. The statue was unveiled by the Secretary of State for War, the Rt. Hon. J.B. Seely, who is seen giving his address.

THE "SIR SAMUEL SADLER" STATUE,
VICTORIA SQUARE, MIDDLESBOROUGH.

35. A view of the statue after the event, standing elegantly in Victoria Square. The villas in the background have now been replaced by the Cleveland Centre. Newton Street ran down the side of the residence shown.

VICTORIA PARK, &
CARNEGIE LIBRARY, MIDDLESBROUGH.

36. The bandstand in Victoria Park, behind the Town Hall, with the 'Carnegie Library' in the background. The message on the back rail of the seat on the left says: 'Reserved For Old People Only.' The park area had originally been a cattle market, and was later used for various entertainments. It was developed as the Victoria Square, with gardens and bandstand, in 1901, and the Police Band played there regularly in the first two years. The Library was opened in 1912, the cost being met almost entirely by the Andrew Carnegie Foundation.

Victoria Square and Town Hall, Middlesbrough.

37. Another view of the Victoria Square and Town Hall area, in the RSK handpainted series of postcards. Probably about 1910. The foundation stone of the new Town Hall was laid in 1883, and the building was completed in 1888. Designed by G.G. Hoskins — who won an open competition with his entry — the Town Hall was officially opened on 23 January 1889 by the Prince (later King Edward VII) and Princess of Wales. Elaborate celebrations followed the opening.

Albert Road with Victoria Park. *Middlesborough*

38. A view at the junction of Albert Road and Grange Road. A smart young man crosses the road to the right, wearing a straw boater and 'plus four' trousers. Again, taken about 1910.

10540—11   HUGH BELL'S SCHOOL, MIDDLESBROUGH.   ROTARY PHOTO. E.O.

39. A clear view of the Hugh Bell Schools, taken about 1910, from Albert Road, with Victoria Park to the left. Repairs to the tram tracks are under way, but judging from the downed shovel and unattended wheelbarrows, it must have been the tea break! The school site is now occupied by the Teesside Law Courts.

40. A school photograph of the Standard 2 form in the Hugh Bell Junior School, taken in 1910. It was not always the custom to include both boys and girls in the same group photo. The teacher was a Miss Bowman. I wonder how many of these children are still alive and living in Middlesbrough.

41. The High School building was opened in 1877, being the result of an initiative by a group of industrialists who had first met to plan such a venture in 1870. The owners of the Middlesbrough Estate gave the land to the School Trustees. The school developed rapidly, and the running of the school was passed over to the Corporation in 1899. The last pupils left the premises in 1959, but part of the building is still standing, and is used by the Teesside Polytechnic.

MIDDLESBROUGH HIGH SCHOOL. Art Room.

42. An industrious scene in the Art Room at the Middlesbrough High School. The pupils are sketching a model of a contemporary tipper truck. Above the master at the back of the room is an exhortation which reads:

Resemble not the slimy snail
Who with its filth records its trail.
Let it be said that where you've been
You left the face of Nature clean.

43. A charming view taken on Empire Day about 1912, with a couple who are believed to be the Mayor and Mayoress being greeted by two children with presents, and by a guard of honour formed by some very early Boy Scouts. A policeman holds open the door of a particularly elegant chauffeur driven vehicle. The venue is thought to be the school yard of one of the central Middlesbrough schools.

New Bus Station, Middlesbrough

44. The Exchange Bus Station, taken about 1926. Several bus companies used the terminus, including Middlesbrough Corporation, United, and various independents. The United bus on the right – an AEC bound for Redcar – would be in brown and yellow livery at that time, when that company's headquarters were still based at Lowestoft.

45. Carriages awaiting their passengers outside the Post Office in Exchange Square in 1910. Young boys sit on the low wall surrounding the statue of Henry Bolckow, waiting for something to happen. The Post Office building was opened in 1879, but was finally closed some ten years ago. The building still stands, however. The statue was unveiled on 6 October 1881, on the town's Jubilee Day, by Lord Cavendish. Bolckow was born in Germany in 1806, made his first fortune in Newcastle where he met John Vaughan, and they both came to Middlesbrough in 1840. They were to make a major impact on the industrial development of the town. The statue was moved to Albert Park in 1925, when the area was developed as a bus station.

MIDDLESBROUGH POSTAL BAND.

46. A typical brass band photograph from just before the Great War, showing the Post Office Brass Band.

47. Not quite the present idea of your local neighbourhood 'pub', the imposing 'Star and Garter' used to stand near the bottom of Marton Road, not far from the old Post Office in Exchange Square. The building is certainly a memorial to the Victorian period of elegant building in Middlesbrough, and this view was probably taken in the 1920's.

48. A nostalgic look at the bottom end of Marton Road, from the junction with Corporation Road which is to the left. The old Post Office and Railway Station lie in the distance, and all the property on the right has now disappeared. The tram lines are clearly visible. The hotel on the corner — the Borough — ist still there today. A vehicle belonging to 'Chapman's — Fish Merchants' is in the centre, and a large removal van from Jonathon Garbutt Ltd. is parked half way down on the right.

SADLERS FIRE AT MIDDLESBRO   COPYRIGHT   AMERICAN STUDIO 1906

49. The reputation of this being an area with sometimes hazardous industries goes back a long way. Here is graphic evidence, with a big fire at the chemical works of Sir Samuel Sadler in Cargo Fleet Road in 1906, where about 500 men were employed. The card was sent to Norfolk in May 1906, with the message: *Dear Aunt, I thought you would like this card. It will give you a little idea what the fire was like.* The first two motor fire engines arrived in Middlesbrough in 1911, and were named 'Sir Samuel Sadler' and 'Lady Sadler', since they were the Mayor and Mayoress in that year.

Corporation Road, Middlesbrough

50. Corporation Road, with an open-top tram, and the Corporation Hotel in the distance. The Empire Theatre is on the left. The grocer's shop to the right was the premises of Robert Dennis.

51. Taken from an advertising card which has survived from the time when a very young Charles Chaplin visited the Empire Theatre in Middlesbrough. Charlie is fourth from the right in the centre row.

Corporation Road, Middlesbrough

52. Corporation Road in 1908, with open top trams and a cart load of hay in the distance. The Empire Palace of Varieties on the right of the picture was opened in 1899, and seated 1500. The celebrated Lily Langtry appeared at the opening performance. In spite of many different uses since the 1950's, the Empire still survives. The building on the left, with bowfronted ground floor windows, is the old Central Hotel which was adjacent to Hinton's Café.

53. A charabanc outing with a mixed party about to set off on a pleasure trip. Probably taken along North Ormesby Road, from an upstairs window across the street, and dated about 1922. The buses belonged to Harrisons, and were nicknamed 'Primus' and 'Sumus'.

54. Off for the day! A gentlemen's charabanc outing, by courtesy of Messrs. T.O. Harrison, whose offices were in Cleveland Street in old Middlesbrough. The bus is named the 'Erimus'. Was it a day out to the coast, or a fishing trip, or a day at the races? There is an air of jollity on the faces of the occupants. The view would be a good one from that height. Note the solid tyres!

55. An interesting view of the North Ormesby Road Toll Bar cabin, with the railway crossing just beyond, and an open top tram standing at the tram terminus. Taken about 1910. The joint owners of this Toll Bar were the Owners of the Middlesbrough Estate Ltd. and J.W. Pennyman Esq. of Ormesby Hall, and its period of operation was from 1854 to 1916.

The Floods, 1903 (The Toll Bar. North Ormesby).

56. Sent to a young lady in Whitby in March 1904, this postcard graphically captures the scene near the North Ormesby Toll Bar when floods struck the town in the previous year. A faithful horse enables eleven young men to keep their feet dry! It looks as though the Toll Bar keeper had decided to have the day off in view of the adverse weather conditions.

Cottage Hospital, North Ormesby, showing new Cochrane Wing.

57. The Cottage Hospital at North Ormesby was the first purpose built hospital in the Middlesbrough district. It opened in 1861, and the cost of £2,646 was raised by public subscription. Workmen later made voluntary weekly contributions of a halfpenny to help fund its operating costs. The Cochrane Wing, donated by the iron manufacturers of Cargo Fleet, was added in 1879, doubling the accommodation at a further cost of £2,400. From 1902, with much additional development having by then occurred, the buildings were simply known as the North Ormesby Hospital. (The hospital closed in September 1981, with the opening of the new South Cleveland Hospital, and has since been demolished.) Evidently the grounds were kept in good order!

58. A classroom view of the North Ormesby Junior Girls School, taken about 1905. Not a smile to be seen, but no doubt there were not many discipline problems either.

59. Taken at the Cargo Fleet Toll Bar in South Bank Road, shortly before the abolition of the Middlesbrough Toll Bars on 31 July 1916. Lord Furness had been the owner of this Toll Bar from 1908. It controlled the Cargo Fleet to Ormesby Village road, and had existed from about 1875. The charge for a two horse wagon was 8d.

60. An early form of powered transport paying the toll at the Cargo Fleet Toll Bar. The vehicle above has an 8 miles per hour speed restriction publicly displayed. It belonged to the firm of Fred Robinson, of Stamp Street, Stockton.

NEW FURNACES, CARGO FLEET. No713.

61. Sent by a young girl to friends near Bishop Auckland, this postcard illustrates the contemporary craze for sending cards: *I hope you will like this one. Thanks for yours. Have you one like this – I have forgot.* The scene is hardly the modern idea of a pleasant greetings card, but to the industrial archeologist such a card is a real 'find'. The rail wagons carry the Bolckow Vaughan and Co Ltd. title. Baron Furness gained a controlling interest in the Cargo Fleet Iron Company in 1900, demolished the old furnaces, and by 1906 had built the first integrated iron and steel plant in the area. The card clearly dates from about that time.

Cargo Fleet Iron Works, Southbank.

62. There were many postcard views of the earlier ironworks, but this is perhaps one of the more interesting of those taken of the Cargo Fleet Works, with a rake of specialised railwagons drawn into a siding.

63. A reminder of the housing conditions which were typical for many in the town areas as recently as about 70 years ago. This view is of Jackson's Terrace, off Normanby Road in South Bank, and was taken in 1910. It gives us some idea of how far housing provision has moved during the intervening years.

Station South Bank.

64. A fine view of the Railway Station at South Bank, with station staff and a policeman in the foreground, and two elegant ladies with a small child in the distance. The card is postmarked 1911. Good railway station postcards are now quite valuable.

65. A visit to the North East coast by King George V and Queen Mary occurred in June 1917, at a time when keeping morale high was a necessary part of the national war effort. The King and Queen are seen arriving on 14 June at South Bank Railway Station, on their way to visit the shipyard of the Smith's Dock Company Ltd.

66. Part of the visit involved passing through the rivet store at the Smith's Dock Shipyard, where the men touched their caps as the King (centre) passed by, conducted by the Chairman, Mr. Launcelot E. Smith. Some of the shipyard girls can be seen in the rear centre, admiring Queen Mary and her elegant hat.

RAILWAY STATION & ZETLAND ROAD, MIDDLESBROUGH.

67. The Middlesbrough Railway Station about 1910, taken from an unusual angle — from the end of Sussex Street, looking towards Zetland Road, with the Grand Hotel to the right. Street vendors can be seen in the foreground, and a horse-drawn cab is to the left. The Station buildings were seriously damaged by bombs in the last war, and look quite different now with the loss of the arched roof and provision of modern offices.

Railway Crossing, Middlesbrough

68. The railway crossing linking Sussex Street and Linthorpe Road. The railway has divided the town into two ever since the coming of the tracks. The old town lies 'beyond the tracks', in the distance. The buildings across the railway include the Sussex and Crown Hotels.

69. A very fine view of the Corpus Christi procession passing along Sussex Street from the area of the Roman Catholic Cathedral and the old town, and moving over the railway crossing into Linthorpe Road. Hundreds of young women and girls can be seen, and great public interest is evident. Taken in the late 1920's.

RAILWAY STATION MIDDLESBROUGH

70. An early view of the Railway Station, postmarked 1904. A small station was built on this site in 1847, at which time the residents of the old town were amazed at placing a station so far from the town centre! Whilst the economic advantages of having the station were self evident, the drawback to the design was that the railway line was gradually to cut the developing town in two. The view is taken from the junction of Linthorpe Road and Zetland Road, again illustrating the original layout of the station buildings. The station as seen here cost £100,000 to build in 1877.

71. A splendid group photograph of the railway staff at Middlesbrough Station in 1915. Even the station cat is included on the lap of someone in the front row! The train on the right is meanwhile kept waiting. Presumably the gentlemen in the middle of the front row include the station master.

72. A fine view outside the Railway Station in Albert Road, with various forms of transport in evidence: the bus to Grove Hill, a tram going to the Transporter Bridge, an L.N.E.R. horse and cart, a hand barrow in the left foreground, two cars in the middle distance on the right, as well as the railway itself. The card was posted in February 1929. The wine merchants – Winterschladen & Co Ltd. – occupied the corner premises for many years. The Albert Railway Bridge – seen in the background – was redecorated very elegantly during 1983.

ROYAL EXCHANGE
(N. & W. FRONT)
AND STATUE TO
THE LATE
JOHN VAUGHAN,
MIDDLESBROUGH.

73. A view of the John Vaughan statue by the Railway Station, with the Royal Exchange building in the background. The statue commemorated the important contribution which Vaughan made – with Henry Bolckow – to the prosperity of the Middlesbrough district. It was unveiled in 1884, but was moved to Victoria Square in 1904, so the postcard pre-dates that event. Vaughan lived at Gunnergate Hall, Marton, from 1858, and died in 1868. The card was posted to a friend at Darlington at 4.45 p.m. on 31 May 1904, and tells us something of the efficiency of the postal service at that time. The message reads: *Gone to Middlesbrough. I am going to Empire (Theatre) so you can go to bed. Leave my supper as it might be late when I get home.*

THE EXCHANGE, MIDDLESBROUGH.

Published by W. ALLAN, The Library, MIDDLESBROUGH

74. A somewhat distorted perspective of the Exchange Building in Albert Road, on an early card posted in 1904. The building has been involved in controversy in recent years, because it stands in the way of a new inner ring road system. It was built for the Middlesbrough Exchange Co Ltd. in 1868, and cost £28,000. The main hall has a magnificent vaulted ceiling with fine decoration. The Iron Market was held there on Tuesdays and Fridays, when prices were settled and large quantities of iron and other merchandise were bought and sold. The card was evidently published by the town library, which at that time was situated in the new Town Hall building.

75. A fine view of the old Hippodrome Theatre of Varieties in Wilson Street. It opened on 17 August 1906, with Florrie Ford as top of the bill on that occasion. The site had previously been a Quaker burial ground, which meant a special nocturnal exhumation procedure when the remains were transferred to the Linthorpe Cemetery. The first 'talkie' film in Middlesbrough was shown here in August 1929. The building closed as a cinema in 1956, but is still in use today. The notices proclaim that film of the Jeffries-Johnson world heavyweight fight is being shown.

The Hippodrome, Middlesbrough

76. Wilson Street during the charity Carnival Week held in 1925. The shop on the right had a special offer on 'The Cosy Pot' – with its 'unbreakable lid and spout'. A number of businessmen are passing the time of day. The sign of the Halifax Permanent Building Society hangs a little way down on the left, and the view is taken from Albert Road.

77. A magnificent decorated tram, used to raise money for local hospital funds during the Charity Carnival which took place in Middlesbrough from 19 to 27 September 1925. The week included processions, dancing, competitions, and fireworks. A massive draw had a house as the major prize. More than £9,000 was raised in total.

78. A fascinating memory of old Middlesbrough – Linthorpe Mews lay between Wilson Street and Corporation Road. Dickson and Benson's elegant shop on the left. In the centre distance are the Wesley Buildings across Corporation Road. Some of the brick walls on the right hand side can still be seen today.

THE WINTER GARDEN, MIDDLESBROUGH. EVENING: THE CROWDED HOUR.

79. Lady Bell established the Winter Garden organisation in 1906, as a club for elderly people, and eight cottages were demolished in Dundas Street and Dundas Mews in order to build the club premises. These were opened in October 1907, with admission costing one penny, and a cup of tea and a biscuit costing another penny. Dominoes, cards, darts, billiards and a library were available. In 1935 the premises were renamed the Dame Florence Bell Gardens. Popular concerts were held, with brass bands, singers and entertainers. The local pianist and international celebrity, Cyril Smith, played there in his early days. The premises were open from 9.00 a.m. to 10.00 p.m. and the organisers were frequently appealing for funds.

80. An interesting view taken at the junction of Linthorpe Road and Corporation Road, looking north down Linthorpe Road towards the Railway Station. Taken about 1910. Collingwoods the jewellers are on the right hand corner, and the old King's Head Hotel is to the left, on the site which later became Newhouses Corner, and which is now Debenhams.

81. The same corner a few years later, when a smart new building had been erected for Newhouses, the drapers. The big Wesleyan Chapel is on the immediate right, behind the railings. Although the road traffic remains largely horse-drawn, a notice on a lamp standard to the left reads 'Caution — Cross Roads. Drive Slowly.'

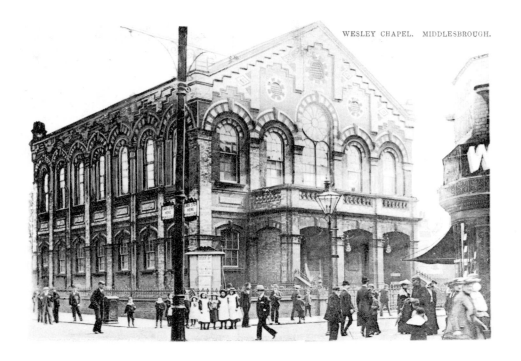

WESLEY CHAPEL. MIDDLESBROUGH.

82. On the site of what is now British Home Stores, at the junction of Corporation Road and Linthorpe Road, the Wesley Chapel was opened in 1863, and seated a congregation of over 800. It was known as 'Big Wesley', and was the finest nonconformist building in the town, with a splendid organ being installed in 1899. A day school with a high reputation was also run from the chapel from 1865 onwards. The building was sold for its present use in 1953. The group of young girls in the centre are clearly intrigued by the camera.

83. Taken looking south down Linthorpe Road, at the junction with Corporation Road. The Wesley Chapel lies to the left, and a large branch of the Manfield & Sons Boot Company is prominent on the right. 'Any foot accurately fitted' proclaims a message on the glass door, and one particular type of boot is advertised at 16/6d. per pair.

LINTHORPE ROAD, MIDDLESBROUGH.

84. A view towards the lower end of Linthorpe Road, with Woolworths store on the immediate left, and 'Red Cross House' – a chemist's shop – next door. The Café Royal is a few doors further down on the same side.

The Corporation Baths, Middlesbrough.

85. The Corporation Baths, situated in Newport Crescent behind the present Binns store, were opened in 1884, and extensions were made in 1901. An old brick pond had previously occupied the site. A swimming bath, 8 cast iron slipper baths and 21 dressing boxes were originally provided, and the first boilers for heating the water had earlier belonged to an old ferry boat! The swimming bath was refilled with fresh water every Monday and Thursday, when admission was sixpence, and the entry charge reduced each day in relation to the state of the water. A treatment system was installed in 1899.

JACK HATFIELD.
ENGLAND'S CHAMPION SWIMMER.

86. One of Middlesbrough's most famous 'sons', Jack Hatfield, won two silver and one bronze medal in the 1912 Stockholm Olympic Games. At the age of 18 years he had won five English Championships, and on four occasions he was a member of the national swimming team at the Olympic Games. His father was the town's Baths Superintendent for some years.

THE NEWLANDS CONVENT, MIDDLESBROUGH.   The old "Newlands Hall."

87. Newlands Hall had originally belonged to Sir H.G. Reid, the founder of the North Eastern Daily Gazette. In the 1880's the Nuns of the Faithful Companions of Jesus rented the property as school premises, and they finally purchased the building in 1896, when it became known as St. Mary's Newlands Convent. It was later extended, and operated both as a Convent and as a Roman Catholic girls school for pupils of 11-16 years until 1965. The building was later demolished. On the back of the postcard is a printed message: *May God bless your undertakings and grant your desires, and may all your days be passed beneath His Divine Shelter.*

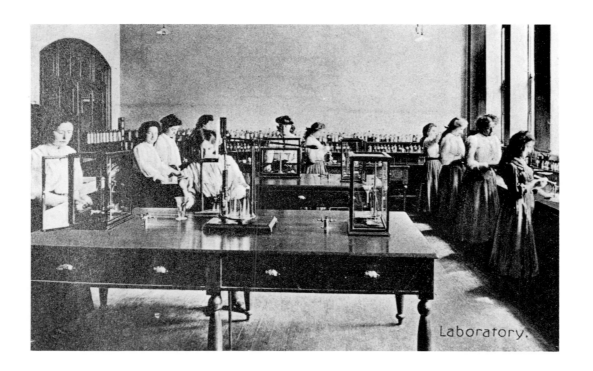

Laboratory.

88. 6th Form science at the Newlands School, Borough Road, about 1910. The photograph comes from a contemporary brochure concerning the school, and makes it clear that the sciences were not denied to young ladies. The laboratory appears to be very well equipped.

89. The Roman Catholic Church in Middlesbrough has a very long history — with the first small chapel dating from 1838 — and there have been many churches and schools serving their followers, as well as the Cathedral in Sussex Street, which was built in 1878. One of my own first memories of Middlesbrough, in 1962, was of the impressive Corpus Christi procession through the town. This colourful event was introduced in 1925, taking place on the Sunday after the feast of Corpus Christi, and the above view of the resplendent clergy was taken on 6 June 1926.

PROCESSION OF THE BLESSED SACRAMENT AT MIDDLESBRO' JUNE 6th 26.

Coughlan Photo R Stokesley

90. Another view of the Corpus Christi procession in 1926, with the young children, their hands clasped as in prayer, being watchfully guided. Crowds are gathered on the pavements. The young girls wear their veils and white dresses, and the boys wear white sashes. A banner is carried in the background. A local photographer from Stokesley — Patrick Coughlan — recorded the event.

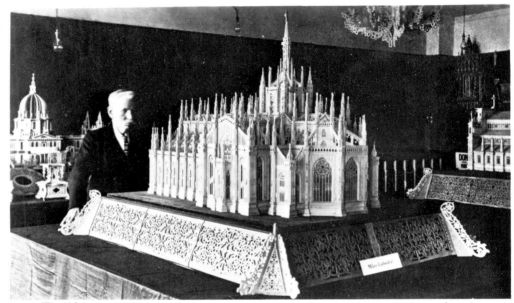

The Maker and Milan Cathedral. Scale. 1 in 100. Over 8.000 pieces. 5 years' work

91. An unusual Middlesbrough item. Richard Old was born in Staithes about 1856, but lived nearly all his life in Middlesbrough. He served an apprenticeship as a cabinet maker, and earned his living as an organ builder. From the age of 25 he built a series of elaborate wooden models, and during a period of 32 years constructed a total of 760 of them in his spare time, often working through the night. He lived in Ruby Street, off Borough Road West, and conducted the famous Cleveland Choral Party of 60 singers for many years. He was also the choir master and organist at the Baptist Church in Marton Road. He died in 1932. His models were exhibited all over Britain, including the Central Hall Westminster in 1931. Another exhibition occurred locally a few years ago at the Preston Park Museum.

92. The head of an impressive procession which took place on Saturday morning, 30 May 1925. Taken on Linthorpe Road, the occasion was the funeral of probably the most well-known of Middlesbrough's clergy over the generations – Father J.S.L. Burn of All Saints Church. He was instituted in 1884, but his High Church practices caused great controversy in church circles. His refusal in 1900 to abandon the use of incense caused All Saints to be placed under a ban by the Archbishops of Canterbury and York. The ban lasted 25 years, and no Bishop was allowed to visit the church, nor were confirmation candidates allowed.

93. The horse-drawn hearse at Father Burn's funeral, which is followed by a group of nuns, and further carriages. Some of the gentlemen in the crowd raise their hats in respect. The Elite Cinema, opened less than two years earlier, can be seen in the background. Father Burn did heroic work in the community during the 1900 smallpox epidemic, and a'so amongst the poor in the subsequent decade when distress and poverty arose from successive trade depressions.

Linthorpe Road   *Middlesbrough*

*You might write while I am here as I intend
staying until monday they are all well & wishes
to be remembered to you all ...*

The Wrench Series No. 4120 — Printed in Saxony

94. An early view of Linthorpe Road, the card being posted in South Bank in 1903. The tram is approaching the camera, heading towards Linthorpe Village, and the view is taken at the junction with Princes Road to the left, and Southfield Road to the right. Pybus' grocer's shop features prominently in the centre, and St. George's Congregational Church can just be seen on the extreme left.

GRAND OPERA HOUSE, MIDDLESBROUGH.   No 710.

95. The Grand Opera House was built on land previously used for fairs and amusements, known as 'Swatters Carr', at the junction of Linthorpe Road and Southfield Road. The Cleveland Agricultural Society had held their annual show here as early as 1879. The Opera House, costing £38,000, was opened by Samuel Sadler M.P. on 7 December 1903. Amongst the nine lock-up shops incorporated in the building was the Grand Oyster Saloon. Live performances were replaced by conversion to the Gaumont Cinema in March 1931. The cinema closed in February 1964, and the building was later demolished, to be replaced by a modern office building – 'Midland House'.

"DISTRESS DINNERS AT THE GRAND OPERA HOUSE MIDDLESBROUGH.
FEB., MAR., APR., 1908.

96. Economic depression in 1907 and 1908 led to thousands of ironworkers being on the verge of starvation at a period when there was no help from the State. There were demonstrations in Middlesbrough, and the Corporation created many temporary jobs to alleviate the position — for example, cleaning out park lakes, and street cleaning. Free dinners and Sunday night concerts were provided at the Grand Opera House, the organisation being undertaken by a Distress Committee. The scene above, in the Spring of 1908, shows rows of children confronted with food bowls, probably in the stage area of the theatre.

St. George's Church, Middlesbrough

97. A view of the Congregational Church of St. George, and St. George's Hall on the left, in Linthorpe
Road, which stood opposite the Grand Opera House. All are now gone. It is possible to see on the left
hand side the scaffolding being used in the construction of the famous terrace of buildings built for
the Cooperative Society, the foundation stone of which was laid in 1897. This card was written in
Hinton's Café, and sent to a friend in Park Lane, whose address is only a few hundred yards from the
view above.

LINTHORPE ROAD, MIDDLESBRO.

No 221.

98. A view of the impressive buildings — now demolished — belonging to the Middlesbrough Coopera-tive Society, in Linthorpe Road. St. George's Church can be seen in the distance on the left, and the Grand Opera House lies opposite it on the right.

99. A carefully posed scene in the boys woodwork room at the Ayresome Schools in Parliament Road, which were opened in 1902. Rows of chisels can be seen on the back wall to the left, and on the right there are diagrams of the annular patterns in various trees. All the boys wear smart white collars, and the master instructs one of the pupils.

THE BORO - V - WOOLWICH

PHOTO GEO. E. TAYLOR
MIDDLESBORO

100. A superb action shot taken in October 1908 at Ayresome Park, when the Boro' and Woolwich Arsenal drew 1-1. The baggy shorts look comical now, but this was no doubt a big game for the town. This postcard, taken by George E. Taylor of Middlesbrough, travelled to Saskatoon, Canada, in a fortnight in 1908, according to the two date stamps on it. The first match at Ayresome Park took place in September 1903. In those early years the great local star was Tim Williamson, capped as England's goalkeeper on seven occasions.

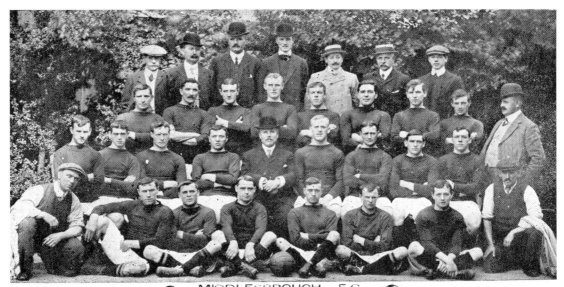

MIDDLESBROUGH F.C.

G W Armitage *Director* W Jones *Director* J H Gunter *Director* A E Forbes *Director* C Hunt *Director* T Bell J C Brown
J Tildsley J Watson R G Williamson A A Hasell A Campbell J Tomlin M Wilson T Dixon J R Smiles
S Aitken J O'Gara W Brawn S Bloomer Lieut.-Col. Poole, V.D. *Ch.* Alf Common *Cp.* F Wilcox J Thackeray T Wilson
J Bingley W Barker W Haxby A Aitken R Brown E Verrell J Harkins T Coulston

Photo copyright by R. E. Fairclough, Middlesbrough

101. A group photograph of the Middlesbrough Football Club directors and players. Lieut. Col. T. Gibson Poole was chairman for many years. In 1905 the club paid a record fee of £1,000 to Sunderland for Alf Common, and in the following year bought Steve Bloomer from Derby for £750. This card is probably dated about 1908, and includes both players.

102. The ceremony to unveil the Cenotaph in commemoration of those who died in the Great War. More than 3,000 names are recorded on the bronze nameplates. The impressive parade of servicemen and civilians, held on 11 November 1922, was inspected by the Lord Lieutenant, Sir Hugh Bell, before marching from the Town Hall to the Albert Park entrance. The Deputy Mayor, Councillor J.G. Pallister, unveiled the Cenotaph, and two blind soldiers unveiled the tablets carrying the names of the fallen. The tablets are on the special park walls to the rear.

SIR ARTHUR DORMAN BART & LADY DORMAN.

103. Sir Arthur Dorman, who died in 1930. He was born in Kent in 1848, and came to Richardson Johnson's South Stockton Yorkshire Ironworks about 1870. He rapidly developed his own businesses, however, and by 1879 had leased the Britannia Works, purchasing it in 1882 in partnership with Albert Long. Many other works were to follow, including the Port Clarence and the Newport Iron Works. In 1901 he offered, as a memorial to his son killed in the Boer War, the provision of a Natural History Museum, initially to house the Sir Alfred Pease collection of African game. The Dorman Museum was opened on 1 July 1904, the assistant curator — who later became famous for his work and writings — being Frank Elgee.

PARK GATES,MIDDLESBROUGH.

104. Posted a few months before the outbreak of war in 1914, this scene gives a good idea of some of the prevailing fashions, set in a framework of the ornamental gates leading into Albert Park. The elaborate clock was presented by Alderman Thomas Sanderson in 1900. The gates had been purchased by Mr. Henry Bolckow at an exhibition in York in 1867, and the Park itself, which cost Bolckow £30,000, was donated to the town by him at a ceremony on 11 August 1868, when the opening was undertaken by Prince Arthur, later the Duke of Connaught. The park was named after Queen Victoria's consort, who had died in 1861, and the opening day was marked by many special events, including a huge procession, and a banquet and ball at Marton Hall – Mr. Bolckow's house – in the evening.

General Sir Leslie Rundle unveiling the South African Soldiers Memorial, Middlesborough June 7th, 1905.

105. The Boer War lasted from 1899 to 1902, and the swinging fortunes of the conflict created great anxiety and excitement in Middlesbrough, particularly the relief of Mafeking, when the British garrison had held out from October 1899 until May 1900. Church bells rang out and bonfires were lit in the streets. The obelisk in memory of the fallen in the South African Wars was unveiled in Albert Park on 7 June 1905 by Lieut.-General Sir Henry Leslie Randle. He can be seen just to right of the monument. It was provided largely by a public subscription organised by the 'Evening Gazette'.

106. Nazareth House — the 'Catholic Orphanage and House for the Aged Poor' (as described in a directory of 1887) — on Park Road North, next to Albert Park. This building dates back to 1906, but the building beyond it was opened in 1884. About 50 of the younger girls can be seen standing in the right hand group, and about 25 older girls are on the left. The card is postmarked 7 December 1907. The Home is run by the Poor Sisters of Nazareth, and it still continues to do great work with the help of voluntary support.

MIDDLESBROUGH SOLDIERS
ARE DOING _THEIR_ DUTY!

PTE. TOM DRESSER.
V.C.

NOW IS THE CHANCE FOR MIDDLESBROUGH PEOPLE TO DO THEIRS!

107. A local card to help in raising funds from Middlesbrough citizens for the War effort. Tank Week in Middlesbrough raised £1,957,797 – an amazing total. The tank 'Nelson' visited the town in January 1918. Two local Victoria Cross holders emerged from the Great War – Private Tom Dresser and Private James Smith.

108. Taken on 12 July 1919, when the town had a special day of peace celebrations following the Great War. The town was decorated, a procession assembled at the Town Hall, and the first stop on the victory march was in Park Road South. The Mayor, Councillor Joseph Calvert, received a tank there on behalf of the Corporation. Various events were held later the same day in Albert Park. The party of dignitaries, which includes the Lady Mayoress, must have had problems in maintaining their dignity whilst negotiating the ladder.

109. A postcard sent as a Christmas greeting, this view of an elegant villa, 'Holmgarth', which still stands in Clairville Road, captures an age when the well-to-do lived no further out of town than the area of Albert Park. A housekeeper and her mistress pose on the balcony, whilst the proud head of household stands in the gateway. The house is on the corner of Egmont Road.

BURGESS WALK. MIDDLESBROUGH.

110. The avenue of trees has matured since this view was taken in 1931. Croydon Road is on the left, and Park Vale Road on the right. At the far end of 'Burgess Walk' lies the junction of Marton Road and Southfield Road. Behind the camera lies the lake in Albert Park, and, nowadays, the Clairville Stadium. A peaceful contrast in a busy industrial town.

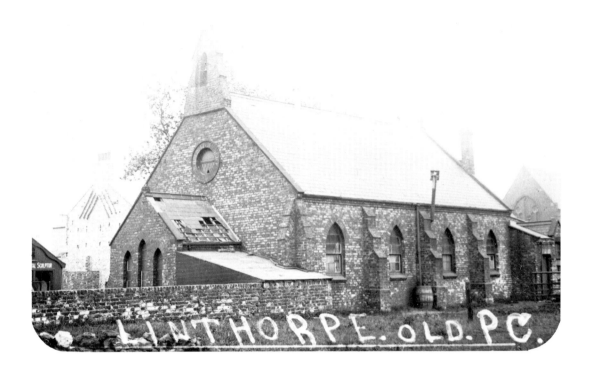

LINTHORPE. OLD. P.C.

111. The original Mission Church of St. Barnabas, built to serve the Linthorpe area in 1874. A modern, larger church was built in 1891, and can just be seen on the right of the picture. This view dates from the turn of the century, when the building was evidently becoming derelict. It lay on what was then called Cemetery Road, which later became St. Barnabas Road.

P.C. 39891 Linthorpe, Linthorpe Road

112. A splendid view taken in Linthorpe Village about 1908, at the top of Linthorpe Road, with the local Post and Telegraph Office on the left – proprietor J.H. Ball. The shop in the shadow on the right has the name J. Creasor above the window. The driver of tram no. 52 stands, as was usual at that time, in the open air, and a street-sweeper can be seen to the right of the tram.

113. Another Linthorpe view with two horse-drawn delivery vehicles as well as a tram. Taken in 1909.

No 8

The Crescent, Linthorpe. Middlesbrough.

R. S. K. Series. - "Handpainted" Copyright.

114. The Crescent, Linthorpe, with two forms of transport in evidence. It was clearly very much a fashionable district, which was well out of the town centre at the time. Taken about 1910.

NEWPORT AND CORPORATION ROADS, MIDDLESBROUGH

115. A close-up on the right of the old Binns' store on Newport Road. 'Men's Outfitters, Milliners, Dressmakers, Hosiery' reads the sign above the shop windows. There were clearly fewer traffic problems fifty years ago! Note the elegant lamp standard.

NEWPORT ROAD, MIDDLESBROUGH

116. This view was published by the firm of Binns, and shows their original shop which accidentally caught fire and was gutted in March 1942. Also on the right is the Grand Electric Theatre, which opened in 1911 and closed in 1960. On the immediate left is the Carlton Billiard Saloon and the Carlton Hall. Further down the row can be seen the 'Oyster Rooms'.

Newport Road, Middlesbrough

117. Postcard views along Newport Road are not too common. The North Riding Infirmary — opened in 1864 — is on the immediate right, with Hartington Road just beyond the two gentlemen in the long coats (newspaper sellers?). The tram is open top, and a notice on the pole in the middle distance urges vehicles to drive slowly through the town. What was the name of the public house on the left of the picture?

Newport Road. Middlesbrough.

118. This card shows St. Paul's Church – built in 1871 – in the distance, with Parliament Street off to the right and Unthank Street off to the immediate left, leading to Cannon Street. Wedgwoods, the grocers, carry a large 'OXO' sign on the end wall of their premises. The tram is open top. The last tram car on the North Ormesby to Stockton route ran in December 1931.

119. Perhaps no collection of scenes from town life would be complete without a view of a corner fish and chip shop. This one was at the junction of Cannon Street and Derby Street, and must have been taken about 1905. An advertisement in the window recalls Garnett's mineral drinks, and there are several vinegar bottles in evidence on the shop counter. The shop was open every evening of the week.

120. Preparatory work for the approach road to the Newport Bridge, with the Newport railway halt in the foreground. Taken in 1931, with St. Cuthbert's Church — opened in 1901 — in the distance. Two of the terraces of houses in the left centre of the view were to be demolished in order to make room for the approach road.

121. Looking in the opposite direction towards the river, with the two terraces now demolished — the left hand side of Samuelson Street (which is on the right) and the right hand side of Calvert Street (which is on the left). Some idea of the major civil works involved in building the Newport Bridge can be gained from this graphic view. Sixty-one houses were demolished, and the families involved were re-housed on the Whinney Banks estate.

122. The Duke and Duchess of York, having opened the Newport Bridge on 28 February 1934 by pressing an electric switch which caused the vertical lifting span to descend to road level, then crossed the bridge both ways in an open-backed Rolls Royce before driving on to the Town Hall for lunch. They were later to become King George VI and Queen Elizabeth, the latter now being the Queen Mother.

123. A fine view of the Newport Bridge, with a typical (for the time) Middlesbrough landscape. Some of the buildings of the Newport Iron Works are framed by the bridge. This view was taken by W. Haig Parry soon after the date of the opening, and some ten years after the decision had been made to proceed with building the bridge. It was the first vertical lift bridge to be built in this country, and the heaviest of its type in the world. The lifting span and its counter balance weigh 5,400 tons. The bridge can be raised 99 feet, and the supporting towers are 200 feet high. The bridge, built by Dorman Long, cost £512,000.

Newport Iron Works, Middlesbrough

124. An impressive view of the old Newport Iron Works, not far from the Newport Bridge and on a site lying between the river and the railway line. The Works was taken over by Dorman Long in 1917, and closed in 1930.

125. Taken in 1908, this view of the Fever Hospital or Sanatorium in West Lane shows the Matron in the elegant gardens with her two dogs. Originally opened in 1872, the premises were frequently being extended as a result of various epidemics – smallpox (including 1890; 1892; 1898-684 cases), scarlet fever (627 cases in 1893) and typhoid fever (1890). The same building is still operating as the West Lane Hospital. A small floating hospital moored in the river was also used for a number of years for cases of highly contagious diseases, from 1886.

THE FLOATING HOSPITAL—(The Tees Port Sanitary Authority)
Visited by the Missions to Seamen Chaplain and literature distributed

126. The floating isolation hospital on the River Tees. This was used in conjunction with the West Lane fever hospital, and the above version was provided in 1895. It was anchored on the north side of the river half a mile below the Eston Jetty, and was used particularly during smallpox epidemics. An earlier floating hospital aboard the brig 'Remembrance' had operated from 1886.

127. A view in the Linthorpe Art Pottery, with the gentleman standing in a hole on the right turning the potter's wheel. A number of pots stand on the left, awaiting firing. The pottery operated between 1879 and 1889, and was situated in the area of the present Northern Dairies depot in Askwith Road, Linthorpe. Genuine Linthorpe ware in good condition is now very collectable, if you can find it.

128. A close-up of the exterior of the Olympia roller skating rink in Oxford Road, Linthorpe, on a card posted in 1910. The building was later used for a short period as a Corporation Transport Depot and for the assembling of new trams, before becoming a commercial garage. It is still standing today, although yet again undergoing a change of use.

OLYMPIA, MIDDLESBROUGH.   COPYRIGHT

129. The first roller skating rink opened in Abingdon Road in 1878, but did not survive for more than a few years. The Olympia Rink in Oxford Road was built some years before the Great War — the postcard is dated August 1909. This view could have been taken on the occasion of the opening of the rink — the skaters are smartly dressed, and include a lady on the left hand edge of the group. All are wearing roller skates, but the lady is firmly clutching the gentleman's arm!

130. The bottom deck of a new tram being delivered for assembly at the Oxford Road Garage in 1921. Nine trams of this kind — with covered-in top decks — were built by Hurst, Nelson & Co. of Motherwell in Scotland, and arrived by railway with top and bottom decks, and bogies, as separate items. The garage was only used by the Corporation from 1920 until early 1922. The hauliers seen in the above picture — Thomas Oxley Harrison Ltd. — were the same firm which operated the charabancs illustrated earlier.

131. Taken at the junction of Cambridge Road and Thornfield Road about 1913, this Bristol single decker bus had begun life in 1911 in the Bristol area, and had later been driven north on solid tyres! No. 62 had then been repainted in the colours of the Imperial Tramways Company – red and white – and re-registered locally. Its route is given as 'Exchange and Cambridge Road via Abingdon Road'. The large building in the background is now the Grey House Hotel.

JV 72256

132. Now known familiarly as Kirby College of Further Education, the building began life in 1911 as a girls secondary school. It was opened by Prince Arthur of Connaught (on the same day that he opened the Transporter Bridge), and named after R.L. Kirby, the Chairman of the Education Committee and author of the book 'Ancient Middlesbrough', published in 1900. The building was enlarged on a number of occasions later, but clearly stood in relatively open countryside on Roman Road originally.

133. Not perhaps immediately recognisable, this view is of Acklam Road, taken in 1910, at a time when the road ahead to the south was being widened. The houses stand at the junction with Appleton Road, and opposite them now stands the Roman Catholic Church of St. Francis of Assisi. Green Lane — known in earlier periods as The Green Lane, and Cross Road — lies somewhere in the distance, running off to the left. Traffic conditions have clearly deteriorated in the past 70 years.

ACKLAM HALL.

134. A fine view of Acklam Hall, which has one of the most elegant exteriors of our local buildings, yet which is rarely featured in early postcards. This card was posted by a servant at the Hall to her mother at Heighington in 1913. William Hustler, born in 1655, built Acklam Hall in 1678. He became M.P. for Northallerton, and died in 1730. The Hustlers had become Lords of the Manor of Acklam in 1637, succeeding the Boynton family. The two families together owned the Acklam estate for more than 650 years. Acklam Hall is specially noted for its staircase and superb ceiling plaster work. Middlesbrough Corporation purchased the building and 39 acres of land for £11,500 in 1929, and the first pupils arrived at the new school in 1935.

MARTON BUNGALOW

Nº513.

135. Many local people still refer to the crossroads of Marton Road and Ladgate Lane as 'Marton Bungalow'. The Bungalow was demolished many years ago, but in the days when there were several green fields between Middlesbrough and Marton, walkers and cyclists called at the Bungalow for refreshments. The building was situated on the south side of Ladgate Lane, opposite the Lodge Gatehouse at the corner of Stewart Park.

The Middlesbrough Crescent Cycle Club

Winners of the Pike Pease Cup, Richmond Meet, Season 1908-9.

136. In the age before the motor car extended beyond the very rich, the pedal cycle was a fashionable mode of transport, especially for outings to the countryside. This group photograph was evidently taken at Richmond in 1908/09, with a fine sporting trophy — the Pike Pease Cup — in the foreground. How the Middlesbrough Crescent Cycle Club achieved this success is not clear. The forms of dress being worn do not look appropriate to cycling in all cases.

137. Built for Mr. H.W.F. Bolckow as his private residence, Marton Hall was constructed in 1853. It was a magnificent house, with marble staircase and containing many valuable works of art. After standing empty for a period, the Hall and grounds were bought from Bolckow's descendants in 1923 by Councillor T.D. Stewart, a former mayor, and presented to the town. He formally opened the park in 1928, naming it after himself. The Hall was demolished in 1960.

138. The Rudds Arms at Marton in 1907. The terrace houses still remain as a prominent feature of older Marton, but the pub has been completely rebuilt on an adjacent site. Again, the lack of road traffic is conspicuous by comparison with the present morning journey into Middlesbrough.

Ormesby Bungalow, near Middlesbrough

139. The Ormesby Bungalow, like the Marton Bungalow, provided recreation and refreshment facilities for the district. A notice by the steps proclaims dancing every Wednesday, and this view was taken in 1920. The building was situated in Ormesby Village, and later became the basis of a garage and petrol filling station.

TOWN HALL, MIDDLESBROUGH.

WITH LOVE
from
Middlesbrough.

140. Obviously the right card with which to conclude this selection. How could the heart not be touched by such a tender greeting! Yet again a by-gone age is captured by the photographer, as a pony and trap carrying two elegant ladies moves across Albert Road by the Victoria Park.